CALMING

THE STORMS

OF LIFE

BY BETTY TOPE

truth
BOOKS
www.truthbooks.net

ISBN 10: 1-58427-361-5

ISBN 13: 978-1-58427-361-5

www.truthbooks.net

Guardian of Truth Foundation
CEI Bookstore
220 S. Marion, Athens, AL 35611
1-855-49-BOOKS or 1-855-492-6657
www.truthbooks.net

TABLE OF
Contents

Lesson One: LONELINESS 5

Lesson Two: REBELLIOUS CHILDREN 9

Lesson Three: UNFAITHFULNESS IN MARRIAGE 12

Lesson Four: REJECTION BY GOD 16

Lesson Five: CHURCH TROUBLES (1): When Church Leaders Fall Away 20

Lesson Six: CHURCH TROUBLES (2): Divisions In The Church 23

Lesson Seven: ON THE ROAD AGAIN: Moving Away From Family & Friends 27

Lesson Eight: FINANCIAL DIFFICULTIES 31

Lesson Nine: CIVIL AND POLITICAL UPHEAVAL 35

Lesson Ten: LOSS OF HEALTH 38

Lesson Eleven: DEATH OF A LOVED ONE 41

Lesson Twelve: WIDOWHOOD 45

Lesson Thirteen: FACING OUR OWN DEATH 49

Foreword

Everyone is overwhelmed at times by the circumstances of her life. Because we are human, we suffer disappointments, disease, death, betrayal, humiliation, loss, rejection, and persecution. I call these the Storms of Life. At times we may seem to handle our "storms" just fine. At other times we are like the fishermen on the Sea of Galilee, overwhelmed by the angry waves, afraid and lost.

As Christians we may then feel guilty that we are not stronger, guilty when our faith is weak. It is my prayer that these studies will reinforce what we have already learned from God's word, perhaps give us some new knowledge and perspectives, and give us the tools to overcome our problems and our fears in ways that are pleasing to God.

With grateful thanks
to the many spiritual men and women
who have helped me through the storms of my life.

Note: All scripture quotations are taken from the New American Standard Bible Updated Edition unless otherwise noted.

Betty Tope
Chesterfield, VA

Loneliness

Psalm 68:6a – *"God makes a home for the lonely."*

Among the many trials a Christian faces is the one of loneliness. This feeling of being alone can be brought about by many different circumstances.

The new Christian may feel lonely as she is rejected by family and former friends. It may come as a shock to the new Christian to find that not everyone is happy and excited about her new-found Faith.

FAMILY

Parents may feel hurt and angry to learn their child has rejected the family faith and traditions. Efforts by the Christian to teach her parents are often met with sarcasm and skepticism. The feeling may be, "Who are you to disobey your parents?" "What gives you the right to lecture your elders?" Their attitude may range from indifference and skepticism about your sincerity and motives, all the way to hostility, physical and verbal abuse, and even shunning or putting the Christian out of the house.

Jesus addresses this in Matthew 19:29 – *"And everyone who has left houses or brothers or sisters or father or mother or children or farms for My name's sake, will receive many times as much, and will inherit eternal life."*

We usually think of this scripture in light of those who leave homeland and family to go to a foreign country to preach the gospel, but it equally applies to those who have to give up that close family connection when becoming a Christian.

We need to be patient with family members, especially if we are younger, and treat them with respect. Though the plan of salvation may be very clear to you, others may be reading the Scriptures with eyes clouded by prejudice and misconceptions that take time to overcome. Though some may understand clearly the first time they read Mark 16:16 (*"He who has believed and has been baptized shall be saved; but he who has disbelieved shall be condemned."*) and will immediately request baptism for the remission of their sins, others will need time to think over this new information. They may want to compare it with what their religious leaders have taught them. Gradually, they will begin to question what they have been taught and may eventually become converted. But, in the meantime you may have to stand alone in your family and stand firm for Christ.

You will not be the first or only one who has had to suffer so. Through the ages, men and women of courage have had to stand alone for the cause of Christ.

Do not think that I came to bring peace on the earth; I did not come to bring peace, but a sword. For I came to set a man against his father, and a daughter against her mother, and a daughter-in-law against her mother-in-law; and a man's enemies will be the members of his household.

He who loves father or mother more than Me is not worthy of Me; and he who loves son or daughter more than Me is not worthy of Me. And he who does not take his cross and follow after Me is not worthy of Me. He who has found his life will lose it, and he who has lost his life for My sake will find it (Matt. 10:34-38).

FRIENDS

Upon becoming a New Testament Christian, we may be surprised to find that our former "friends" disappear. When they find we no longer talk like they do, practice the same vile habits they do, go to the same questionable places they do, they usually seek companions elsewhere. We are not the first to experience this. Christians of the first century had the same problem. *"For the time already past is sufficient for you to have carried out the desire of the Gentiles, having pursued a course of sensuality, lusts, drunkenness, carousing, drinking parties and abominable idolatries. In all this, they are surprised that you do not run with them into the same excesses of dissipation, and they malign you"* (1 Pet. 4:3-4).

Fortunately, God has provided us with a whole new family of friends in the church. Our brethren will pray for us, care for us when we are sick, feed us when we are hungry, lift us up when we get discouraged, advise us when we are confused and troubled. Our new family of brethren in Christ truly do become our mothers and fathers, sisters and brothers.

BRETHREN

Theoretically, we should never have to experience loneliness again. But, sometimes our brethren will fail us, too. Close friends may become enmeshed in sin and fall away from the church, go off into religious error, or otherwise become lost to us. We may try to maintain contact with such a one, but the unity of purpose and life is lost. In the words of the prophet Amos, *"Can two walk together, unless they are agreed?"* (Amos 3:3, NKJV).

At such times we may become depressed to the point we feel all alone. We may begin to wonder if anyone else is standing for the Truth. At times like this we should remember Elijah at his low point and the Lord's reply to him (1 Kings 19:13-18). Elijah felt like he was the only person left in Israel who still worshiped the one true God. God chided Elijah in his despair. He commanded him to get busy, and informed him there were 7,000 men in Israel who had not bowed the knee to the idol Baal.

THE REMEDY

This is our remedy for loneliness, too. We have to forget about self and seek out others who may be in need. We may think of brethren and neighbors who are in physical need: those who are ill, depressed, lonely, widowed, separated from family members by war or other causes, lonely college students away from home. As you see to their physical needs with gifts of food, home cleaning or repairs, babysitting, running errands, or the simple gift of a flower from your garden, you will find your own heart lifted and your life full of purpose again. If you are homebound yourself, a telephone call or a note from the heart will bring a smile and a cheer to someone else.

Don't forget to think of the spiritual needs of others. Everyone you come in contact with is in need of the gospel. Try to develop the constant awareness of this need in others. As you walk down the street, as you speak to the clerk at the bank, dry cleaners or grocery store, as you chat with coworkers and neighbors, learn to look past the physical attributes and characteristics of people and see instead a soul crying out for a Savior! Use every opportunity in conversation to teach a biblical truth, invite others to Bible studies and worship services, invite them to a Bible study in your home where you or a more knowledgeable member of the church can teach them God's word and His plan of salvation. The busier we are in doing good unto others, the less time we will have to feel sorry for ourselves.

BLESSED WITH FRIENDS

What about those of us who are not lonely? We may be blessed with a circle of friends and family nearby and have very full social schedules. Thank God for your blessings! But, don't forget those brethren who are not so fortunate. Make room in your life for the friendless, the lonely, and those who are single. Don't always invite couples only to your dinner parties. Include single people, too, and a mix of ages. You will be blessed!

NEWCOMERS TO THE CONGREGATION

We often overlook the new preacher's family and those who have moved into our area from elsewhere. Don't leave it up to them to exercise all the hospitality. They will be thrilled to receive an invitation to your home for coffee/tea or something as simple as popcorn. The important thing is not the food, the size or condition of your home, but the love shown by you.

One of the down sides to moving into a new area is having to locate new doctors, dentists, etc. Consider putting together a welcome package for newcomers (including the new preacher's family). Some suggestions are as follows:

A list of member-recommended facilities such as:

- Doctors
- Dentists
- Hospitals
- Schools
- Hairdressers
- Grocers
- Shopping malls
- Dry cleaners
- Banks
- Realtors

- Mechanics
- Electricians
- Plumbers
- Heating/cooling repairmen

A local map with location of:

- utilities
- government offices

A pictorial directory of members is very helpful. We have included directions from the church building to each member's home in ours.

QUESTIONS:

1. Why are family members apt to reject us when we become Christians?

_____

_____

2. How can we go about teaching them? _____

_____

_____

3. Is it unusual for friends to forsake us as we let God's word transform our lives? _____

_____

4. Name some reasons relationships with brethren become strained or severed. _____

_____

_____

5. List some remedies in overcoming our own loneliness and how we can help others. _____

_____

_____

Rebellious Children

"I hate you!"

"I'm __ years old now and can do what I please!"

"You can't make me!"

"You can't stop me!"

These and many other hurtful things are said to parents by their rebellious teenage children. Some run away or move out. They may become sullen and uncommunicative or sassy and argumentative. They may become arrogant and treat you with disdain. These rebellious ones will choose friends you don't approve of. They will adopt the practices most likely to hurt you, i.e. they may drop out of school if you are an educator, become sexually promiscuous if their father is a preacher, steal if their father is a banker. They will certainly do things you have taught against and don't approve of. Many turn to alcohol and drugs so they will fit in with their peers.

You, as the parent, are stunned to find your sweet, obedient child, with whom you've always had a good relationship, suddenly turn into this monster who is a complete stranger. We are prone to blame our child's rebelliousness on the times we live in, but a study of the Bible will reveal this problem has existed since the days of the first family on earth. Adam and Eve had two sons. Abel was righteous and Cain was disobedient. Had they treated the two boys differently? I doubt it. Had they failed to instill a respect for God and His will in one, while spending time teaching the other? I doubt it. Abel offered his sacrifice by faith (which comes from hearing God's word, Rom. 10:17) while Cain offered what was convenient and what he **thought** would be acceptable to God. We do know Adam and Eve did not always obey God's word, as evidenced by their being driven from the Garden of Eden. (Please read Gen. 3-4:14; Heb. 11:4.)

Both Samuel and Eli were rebuked by God because they failed to correct their ungodly sons. And why did they fail to do so? We are told Eli honored his sons more than he honored God (1 Sam. 2:29; 3:11-13). That shocks us! But how many times do we do the same? When we allow and even accompany our children to sport and scouting events instead of attending Bible study and worship, whom are we honoring? When we encourage them to get jobs that necessitate missing worship or Bible study, whom are we honoring? When we make excuses for their rude behavior, indifference, and wrong doings instead of correcting them, whom are we honoring? When we blame Bible class teachers and other members for driving our children away from serving God, whom are we honoring?

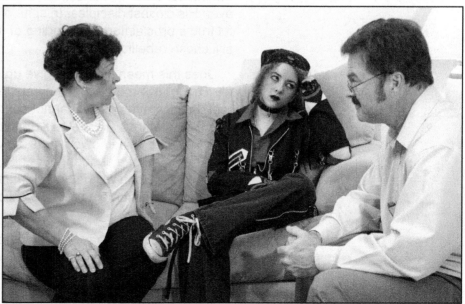

Notes

God has given fathers the responsibility for bringing up their children in the nurture and admonition of the Lord (Eph. 6:4). Paul commends Lois and Eunice for instilling a faith in God and Christ in young Timothy (2 Tim. 1:5). There is no excuse for turning our responsibility over to others. The Jews of old were commanded to teach their children God's word when they were sitting in their house, walking along the pathway, lying down at night, and rising up in the morning (Deut. 6:4-9). In other words, they were to be teaching their children daily, morning, noon and night. It is a full-time job! We start with our little ones showing them the wonders of nature and teaching them about God's part in the creation and His care for us. If others act in an ungodly way to them, we show them what the Scripture has to say about our behavior and response to others. If they are taught error in school or via the media, we counter that with the truth of God's word. There are countless opportunities daily to contrast the teachings of the world with the teachings of the Bible. We show them "the better way."

It is so easy for us to look at other families and think their children are being rebellious or have left the Faith because the parents were perceived by us as too strict or too lenient, did not always do right in God's eyes themselves, etc. When it is our child, however, we are often blind sided and have no idea where this rebellious spirit is coming from. We waste fruitless hours questioning "Why?" We second guess our parenting skills and wonder where we went wrong. We may be embarrassed by the shame and reproach our children are bringing on our family and the church. Little do we know how many other families are going through the same heartache until we begin to share one another's burdens. We can learn much from our older sisters who have dealt with a similar situation.

The truth is, God has given each of us a free will. Cain chose the way of sin and Abel chose the way of righteousness. If after we have taught our children God's word and will for us, have exemplified the joy of Christianity, have been the best example we can be and our child still rejects our authority and will, which in reality is rejecting God, we should not beat ourselves up over it. If we have made mistakes, we should correct them and ask God's forgiveness as well as our children's. Even Christ, the master teacher, the sinless Son of God, did not manage to save all of even His closest disciples. In spite of the miracles performed, the wonderful truths proclaimed, the feeding of the physical and spiritual man, Judas still chose rebellion and sin.

Does this mean we are to give up on our wayward children? Not at all! Though we must insist they abide by our rules while living under our roof, there are things we cannot control. This is a hard lesson for us to learn. As mothers, we feel it is up to us to fix things. That is our job! From birth we have kissed away hurts, solved problems, protected our children from harm. All of a sudden, our child has placed him/herself in a situation where he/she will be hurt spiritually and often physically. We can no longer shield that most precious child from the consequences of his/her actions.

If they choose to leave home rather than abide by our rules, we must assure them of our continual love and desire for their well being and happiness. We can and must keep the lines of communication open and pray for them fervently. Once we have done all in our power to do, we must turn the problem over to God and trust Him for the outcome.

In our grief and despair for our rebellious children, we must not allow that grief to consume us to the neglect of our other children or our service to God. Because of the turmoil in the home, the other children may be frightened, not understanding what is happening. They may feel abandoned by us if all our energies are spent anguishing over their erring sibling. They still need the security of our love, interest, and care for them.

Life must go on while our children wander in their path of sin and debauchery. We still have meals to cook, clothes to wash, and a house to clean. We have other duties to perform, others to teach both by example and word. Our faith in God and service to Him will see us through good times and bad. God will not fail us! When our children come to their senses, it will be a comfort and relief to them to find us in the same place, happy in our service to God.

Husbands and wives usually react differently to these problems. In our hurt and anger one may want to banish the child from home altogether and the other prefer to take a softer approach. Don't allow your disobedient child to drive a wedge between you and your husband. Allow your mate to deal with his hurt and anguish in his own way and talk over your differences in private. Don't present a divided front to the child! Pray together!

As the father of the prodigal son no doubt prayed continually for his son's return and watched the horizon daily, so we should be ready to rejoice and welcome our children home when they are ready. If you are a grieving parent, my earnest prayer is that for you, *"joy cometh in the morning"* (Psa. 30:5).

QUESTIONS:

1. Name some examples from Scripture of disobedient children. _____

_____

_____

2. How serious is rebellion in the eyes of God? See Deuteronomy 21:18-21. _____

3. Who is to blame for a child's rebellion? Give scripture to back up your answer. _____

_____

_____

4. What steps can we take to win back our rebellious child? _____

_____

_____

5. What are some pitfalls the parents of a rebellious child should try to avoid? _____

_____

Notes

lesson 3

Unfaithfulness in Marriage

GOD'S PERFECT PLAN

All of God's laws for mankind are for our good. The first institution ordained by God was that of marriage and the resultant family. God created one woman for one man for life. We read in Matthew 19:4-7 – *"And He answered and said, 'Have you not read that He who created them from the beginning made them male and female, and said, "For this reason a man shall leave his father and mother and be joined to his wife, and the two shall become one flesh"? So they are no longer two, but one flesh. What therefore God has joined together, let no man separate.'"*

There is no more intimate or sacred relationship on earth than that of husband and wife. The home established by the marital couple is meant to be a haven from the onslaughts of the world. The husband has a right to expect love, obedience, and respect in his own home. The wife has a right to expect her husband to love her, cherish her as his own body, and provide for her needs and her well being (Eph. 5:22-32). Children have a right to expect a home filled with love and harmony, where they will learn God's will by Word and example, where they will be taught to respect the rights of others and to be obedient to parental authority. Solid homes build solid communities and solid communities build strong nations. This is God's plan. When we follow His plan, we are most blessed and the happiest of peoples.

What happens when one or both partners in the marriage contract violate the commitment to keep him/herself only to the one to whom he or she is lawfully married?

We sin against God. We sin against our mate. We destroy and disillusion our children. We defile ourselves (1 Cor. 6:18). This is the real picture of sin, not the beautiful picture of Camelot. In that picture, we deceive ourselves into thinking lust is love, adultery is unavoidable, and divorce is in the best interests of all. What a miserable substitute for the happiness and security of the family as God ordained it!

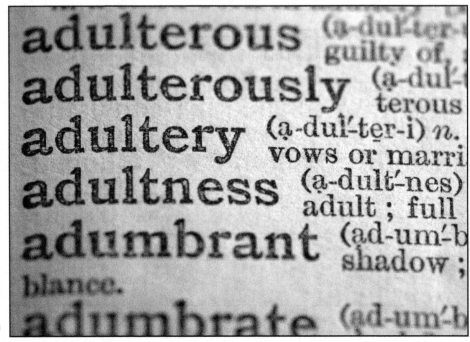

CAUSES OF ADULTERY

What are some of the causes of adultery?

1. Unbelief in God and His word has to be the number one cause. We don't really believe God will punish the adulterer. We don't really believe God was serious in saying I have to live with my husband until death parts us! We greatly lessen the chances of having a cheating husband when

we marry a man who has the same values, beliefs, and commitment to God that we do.

2. Promiscuousness promoted by TV, movies, books, and magazines would lead one to think *everyone* is doing it, so it must be ok. In most of today's fictional love stories, the couple engage in sex on their first date. It has come to be expected. In this country, a white wedding gown used to be the symbol of the bride's purity. Today, it is quite common for a couple to live together several years, maybe have two or three children together before marriage, and for the bride still to get married decked out in a beautiful white gown.

3. All too often our children's role models are people in sports or government and movie stars. Their immoral lives are the worst examples our children can follow. As adults we may give our stamp of approval by voting into office the people known to be immoral and unfaithful to their spouses. We may flock to the movies or the games where the stars have flaunted God's laws with their multiple affairs and marriages.

4. With today's many forms of birth control being freely available in the supermarket, drugstores, and often in schools, there is less fear of pregnancy. To our shame, the option of killing our unborn children, otherwise known as abortion, is also readily available. Murder seems preferable to self control.

ELEMENTS THAT MAY CAUSE US TO SIN

1. Loneliness can get us into trouble. Also, feelings of being unloved and unappreciated by one's husband can put one at risk. If we start feeling neglected by our spouse and sorry for ourselves, we may cast a wishful eye toward someone we perceive as more understanding and more caring. This is *"the grass is greener on the other side of the fence"* syndrome.

2. Idleness and boredom are also pitfalls. As the saying goes, *"Idle hands are the Devil's tools."* We all know what happens to children when they have nothing to do. They will invent all kinds of mischief. The same holds true of adults, if we are not careful. Consider David's sin (2 Sam. 11:1-4). Instead of going to battle with his army, David stayed home and fell into Satan's trap.

3. One of the sinful and often unintentional effects of drinking alcoholic beverages or smoking pot is that it causes one to relax and let one's guard down. Many a naive person has gotten into trouble sexually after having a few drinks or taking drugs.

4. Filling our minds with immoral thoughts is another activity that may lead to immoral actions (Eph. 5:3-7).

ANTIDOTES TO IMMORALITY

1. Concentrate on the needs of others rather than on self. Be busy doing good, teaching and helping others. If we forget self, we are less likely to feel lonely or neglected.

2. Don't compare your husband to other men. Everyone has good and not-so-good attributes. When you compare your husband's weaker

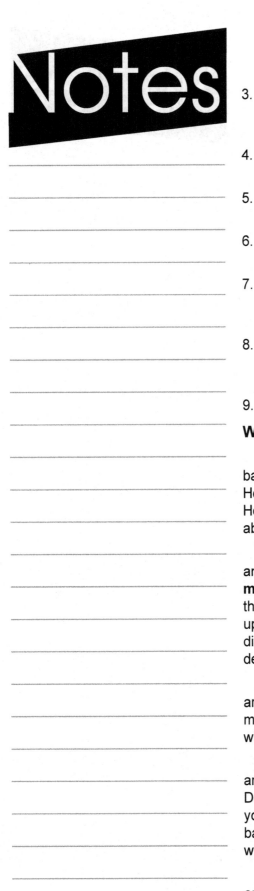

qualities to the good qualities of someone else, you are blind to that man's weaknesses as well. Concentrate on your husband's good qualities. List the things you loved about him before marriage.

3. Make yourself attractive and loveable. The more attractive and loving you are, the more he will want to spend time with you and it will be easier for him to resist the advances of others in the workplace.

4. Spend time together. Go on dates. Try to have an occasional one-night honeymoon. Keep the spark of romance alive.

5. Communicate! Tell your spouse how you are feeling. Chances are he is oblivious to your hurts and longings.

6. Live within your means. The number one cause of arguments in marriage is money – the lack of it, the control of it, the spending of it.

7. Keep alert and sober. Don't flirt with other men. Avoid even the appearance of evil. The heart of your husband should be able to trust in you at all times. See Proverbs 31:11.

8. Flee if necessary. Remember Joseph. If, in spite of all your precautions, you find yourself in a compromising situation and temptation rears its ugly head, FLEE!

9. Think on things lovely, pure, etc. Remember Philippians 4:8

WHAT IF ALL THE ABOVE FAILS?

Sometimes a marriage fails in spite of all efforts to save it. Your husband may have a roving eye and is unwilling to keep himself to you only. He may unintentionally become romantically involved with someone else. He may be away from home and give in to temptation. What are you to do about it?

The Bible gives the innocent partner the right to divorce her husband and marry again (Matt. 19:9; 5:32). Jesus did not say the innocent party **must** divorce her mate, but that she has a right to. Divorce is not always the answer. I have known couples who have worked things out and built up trust again and been very happy. I have also known couples who have divorced and have been miserable. Only YOU, the innocent party, can determine what you can live with.

What if your husband divorces you through no fault of your own? How are you to act? Do not grovel or tell your problems to every stranger you meet. You will drive your friends away and scare away others. You will not win your husband back by whining.

You are still a Princess, the daughter of the King! Hold your head high and determine to live for God. Make a life for yourself in service to others. Do not be bitter or full of hatred for your former spouse. It will only make you miserable and destroy your own life. Do not bad mouth your ex-husband to your children. As they grow older, they will learn for themselves what kind of man their father is.

Don't sit home and brood. Keep up your social life. Don't wait for others to invite you out. They may be hesitant, not knowing how to act. Be friendly. Be cheerful. Invite friends to your home for lunch or tea. Eventually, they will reciprocate. You may need to make new friends if your old ones side with your husband or only want to invite couples. Be prepared for this attitude or it can be devastating.

What should be our attitude toward a fellow Christian going through a divorce? Be supportive. Try not to be judgmental unless we know her to be in the wrong. Don't bad mouth his/her ex. Only the two involved know what happened and sometimes only one of them knows the truth.

QUESTIONS:

1. What is God's plan for marriage and what are some of the resulting blessings? _____

_____

_____

_____

2. What are some of the causes for adultery?_____

_____

_____

3. What can we do to avoid the temptation of marital infidelity? _____

_____

_____

4. How can a marriage be saved when the vows are violated? _____

_____

_____

5. How should the divorced person conduct herself and what should be the attitude of others in the congregation toward that person? _____

_____

_____

_____

Notes

lesson 4

Rejection by God

As bad as it is being rejected by family, friends, brethren, and husband, the worst rejection of all is being rejected by God. Is this possible, you ask? The Scriptures are replete with warnings of just such a rejection. Matthew gives us this warning:

> But when the Son of Man comes in His glory, and all the angels with Him, then He will sit on His glorious throne. All the nations will be gathered before Him; and He will separate them from one another, as the shepherd separates the sheep from the goats; and He will put the sheep on His right, and the goats on the left.

> Then the King will say to those on His right, "Come, you who are blessed of My Father, inherit the kingdom prepared for you from the foundation of the world." . . . Then He will also say to those on His left, "Depart from Me, accursed ones, into the eternal fire which has been prepared for the devil and his angels" (Matt. 25:31-34, 41).

Who are these accursed ones who will be rejected of God and cast into the eternal fires of hell?

Those who don't obey the gospel: " . . . dealing out retribution to those who do not know God and to those who do not obey the gospel of our Lord Jesus. These will pay the penalty of eternal destruction, away from the presence of the Lord and from the glory of His power" (2 Thess. 1:8-9; Mark 16:16).

The immorally sinful: "The acts of the sinful nature are obvious: sexual immorality, impurity and debauchery; idolatry and witchcraft; hatred, discord, jealousy, fits of rage, selfish ambition, dissensions, factions and envy; drunkenness, orgies, and the like. I warn you, as I did before, that those who live like this will not inherit the kingdom of God" (Gal. 5:19-21,NIV); "But for the cowardly and unbelieving and abominable and murderers and immoral persons and sorcerers and idolaters and all liars, their part will be in the lake that burns with fire and brimstone, which is the second death" (Rev. 21:8). "Or do you not know that the unrighteous shall not inherit the kingdom of God? Do not be deceived; neither fornicators, nor idolaters, nor adulterers, nor effeminate, nor homosexuals, nor thieves, nor the covetous, nor drunkards, nor revilers, nor swindlers, shall inherit the kingdom of God. And such were some of you; but you were washed, but you were sanctified, but you were justified in the name of the Lord Jesus Christ, and in the Spirit of our God" (1 Cor. 6:9-11).

- Fornicator
- Adulterer
- Impure and those who practice debauchery
- Idolater
- Sorcerer
- Dabbler in witchcraft
- Hater
- Jealous
- Causer of discord
- Given to fits of rage
- Envious
- Drunkard
- Selfishly ambitious
- Dissenter
- Factious
- Involved in orgies
- And such like
- Unbeliever
- Coward
- Liar
- Murderer
- Effeminate
- Homosexual
- Thief
- Swindler
- Covetous

Unfaithful, lukewarm Christians and those who fall away: Some seem to think once they become Christians there is nothing left for them to do. Some continue to wallow in the same sins they were guilty of before becoming Christians. Others may live morally pure lives but become bench warmers, sitting on the sidelines, never engaging in the battle. They may attend services erratically or attend the Sunday morning worship but none of the Bible studies. Consequently, they don't grow. They never become Bible class teachers, men don't learn to lead singing or lead in prayer, never mind become elder and deacon material. They are easily led into error by false teachers. When temptations or troubles arise, these weak Christians may fall away altogether. Some will simply stop coming to worship. Some will start attending a denomination or a more liberal group that will overlook or condone their sins.

Our Savior warns us of all these attitudes and consequences in the parable of the sower (Luke 8:11-15). "Now the parable is this: the seed is the word of God. Those beside the road are those who have heard; then the devil comes and takes away the word from their heart, so that they will not believe and be saved. Those on the rocky soil are those who, when they hear, receive the word with joy; and these have no firm root; they believe for a while, and in time of temptation fall away. The seed which fell among the thorns, these are the ones who have heard, and as they go on their way they are choked with worries and riches and pleasures of this life, and bring no fruit to maturity. But the seed in the good soil, these are the ones who have heard the word in an honest and good heart, and hold it fast, and bear fruit with perseverance."

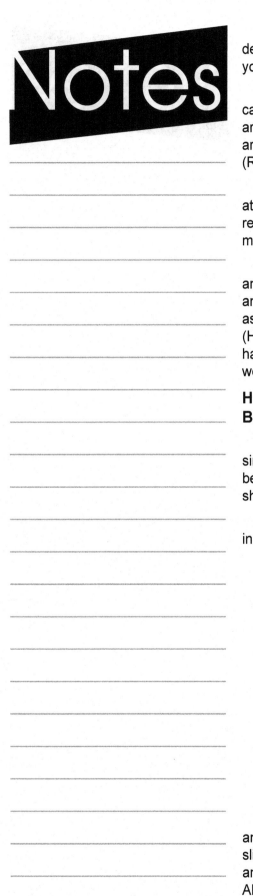

Christians in the church at Smyrna were admonished to be faithful unto death to receive a crown of life. ". . . be faithful until death, and I will give you the crown of life" (Rev. 2:10).

The brethren at Laodicea were warned that their lukewarmness would cause Christ to spit them out of His mouth. "I know your deeds, that you are neither cold nor hot; I wish that you were cold or hot. So because you are lukewarm, and neither hot nor cold, I will spit you out of My mouth" (Rev. 3:15-16).

With all other broken relationships, there is the possibility of reconciliation. Wayward children may mature and come home. Marriages can be repaired, even after divorce. Friends and brethren can come to agreement later in life.

While we have breath, we have the opportunity to repent of our sins and ask God's forgiveness. However, once death claims this mortal body and the soul returns to God, there is no such opportunity. "And inasmuch as it is appointed for men to die once and after this comes judgment" (Heb. 9:27). The book of life is closed until the final judgment day. If we have not obeyed the Gospel and not kept our relationship right with God, we will have to face His final rejection on that day.

HOW CAN WE MAKE THINGS RIGHT WITH GOD AND AVOID BEING REJECTED BY HIM?

The apostle Paul tells us in the letter to the Romans that all have sinned and fall short of the glory of God (Rom. 3:23). God sent His only begotten son, Jesus Christ, to save us from our sins, the cost being His shed blood on the cross.

That same letter to the Romans explains how we are buried with Christ in baptism and raised to walk in newness of life.

> Or do you not know that all of us who have been baptized into Christ Jesus have been baptized into His death? Therefore we have been buried with Him through baptism into death, so that as Christ was raised from the dead through the glory of the Father, so we too might walk in newness of life. For if we have become united with Him in the likeness of His death, certainly we shall also be in the likeness of His resurrection, knowing this, that our old self was crucified with Him, in order that our body of sin might be done away with, so that we would no longer be slaves to sin; for he who has died is freed from sin.

> Now if we have died with Christ, we believe that we shall also live with Him, knowing that Christ, having been raised from the dead, is never to die again; death no longer is master over Him. For the death that He died, He died to sin once for all; but the life that He lives, He lives to God. Even so consider yourselves to be dead to sin, but alive to God in Christ Jesus (Rom. 6:3-11).

If you have already given your life to Christ by repenting of your sins and being baptized for the remission of those sins, but now find yourself slipping back into the world, or your zeal for Christ waning, repent today and ask God's forgiveness. Don't take a chance on being rejected by the Almighty on the Day of Judgment!

QUESTIONS:

1. Will all people go to Heaven? _____ Explain your answer. _____
_____
_____

2. Who will be rejected by God in the Day of Judgment? _____
_____
_____

3. What will keep us from being ushered into Heaven? _____
_____

4. Is it possible for a murderer to be saved? _____ What about the homosexual? _____ What about the abortionist? _____
How? _____
_____

5. What must I do to be saved? _____
_____
_____

Notes

lesson 5

Church Troubles (1):

WHEN CHURCH LEADERS FALL AWAY

FEET OF CLAY

"Make every effort to come to me soon; for Demas, having loved this present world, has deserted me and gone to Thessalonica" (2 Tim. 4:9-10). These, to me, are some of the saddest words recorded in the New Testament. Nearing the end of his life, in prison for the gospel's sake, the great apostle Paul has been forsaken by a former co-worker in the kingdom of Jesus Christ. Demas is spoken of in Colossians 4:14 and Philemon 23, 24 as one of Paul's fellow workers in Rome. Now, in Paul's darkest hour, Demas has forsaken him. Did Demas' faith waver? Did he lose courage? Was he overtaken by fear or lustful temptations? Paul simply says he loved this present world. This once spiritual man, teacher of the Word of God, commended by an apostle, companion of the imprisoned Paul, in the end proved to have feet of clay.

How many church leaders have you known who have succumbed to Satan's wiles and are no longer even worshiping with the saints? Elders, deacons, and preachers who were once respected and looked up to as examples of godly men? Men who worked side by side with you in teaching others? Men who may have been responsible for your own obedience to the gospel?

HOW DID THE DEFECTION OF THESE ONCE GODLY MEN AFFECT YOU?

Were you surprised? (I can't believe brother _____ would do such a thing!) Were you disappointed? (I never in a million years would have thought he would do that!) Were you discouraged? (If a preacher can fall away, what hope do I have?) Did you feel betrayed? (I trusted him completely!)

As a young girl and a young Christian, I visited a girlfriend who happened to be an elder's daughter. While there, her father let out a curse as he hit his thumb with a hammer. Needless to say, I was shocked and disillusioned. From that time on I held him in less esteem. As the years passed, I learned that no one is perfect. Being

appointed an elder does not make one faultless. We all sin. We need not overlook sin in others, but our faith should not depend on the faithfulness of men.

Even our Lord was betrayed by Judas, one of the chosen twelve (Matt. 26:47-49), and forsaken by the apostles when He was arrested (Matt. 26:31). How must the early disciples have felt when they saw their leaders display their feet of clay?

We may feel personally betrayed. After all, these are men we trusted. These are men we held in high esteem. These are men who, outwardly anyway, were men of integrity. They had the ability to teach and preach God's word with conviction and courage. We must remember these men have not only betrayed us but primarily they have sinned against God. Remember Ananias and Sapphira. Though they lied to the brethren and the apostles, Peter said they had lied to God (Acts 5:4).

WHY DO ELDERS, DEACONS AND PREACHERS FALL AWAY?

We tend to ascribe to church leaders special abilities and powers to resist the wiles of the devil, when in reality, they may be under more attack than the rest of us. The devil knows our weaknesses and is ever assailing us. It seems to be a temptation for man that, when elevated to prominence or positions of authority, pride rears its ugly head. We are warned in Proverbs, *"Pride goes before destruction, And a haughty spirit before stumbling"* (Prov. 16:18). We have only to look to politicians and world leaders, prominent actors, and sportsmen and women to see the effect of power and pride on people. The British historian, Lord Acton, stated it well in 1887, "Power tends to corrupt and absolute power corrupts absolutely." Fame, authority, and power tend to cause such a person to feel he or she is above the law, whether civil or biblical law.

The preacher who preaches against fornication and adultery may himself be caught up in this sin. If he has not determined at the outset to never allow himself to be in a compromising position with a woman, he greatly increases the risk of temptation and opportunity to become overtaken in the sin of adultery. Some women see presidents and preachers as a challenge for their sexual prowess. They count it a personal coup to bring down such a man. A godly man will beware of entrapment in counseling unhappy, self-centered women. He may be so taken in by the abuses she is reportedly suffering, the neglect she endures from her husband, and her need for love and affection that he ends up unlawfully supplying her need.

The deacon may be tempted to pilfer from the treasury, not having learned from the example of Judas. He may have a nagging wife who is never satisfied to live within her husband's income. He may buy into the constant sales pitches from the media advertisements that everything we presently own is not good enough. We need newer and better! We *deserve* newer and better!

The young preacher may become so discouraged by the constant denigration, humiliation, and faultfinding of ungodly brethren that he becomes discouraged, sick at heart, and weak and ends up not only leaving the pulpit but leaving the Faith. Should he have been stronger? Yes. Will he be judged for his lack of faith and weakness? Yes. But brethren who criticize every word the preacher speaks and every deed he does or does not do, will have to answer for their actions, too. If the apostle Paul was compelled to admonish fathers not to provoke their children to anger (Eph. 6:4), how much more so will brethren be held accountable for destroying God's servant with the beautiful feet (Rom. 10:15)?

WHAT ARE SOME OF THE FALLOUTS AMONG THE CHURCH WHEN LEADERS FAIL?

We have already discussed how we as individuals can lessen the impact on us personally when leaders in the church sin or fall away. Let me recap. Our faith will stay strong:

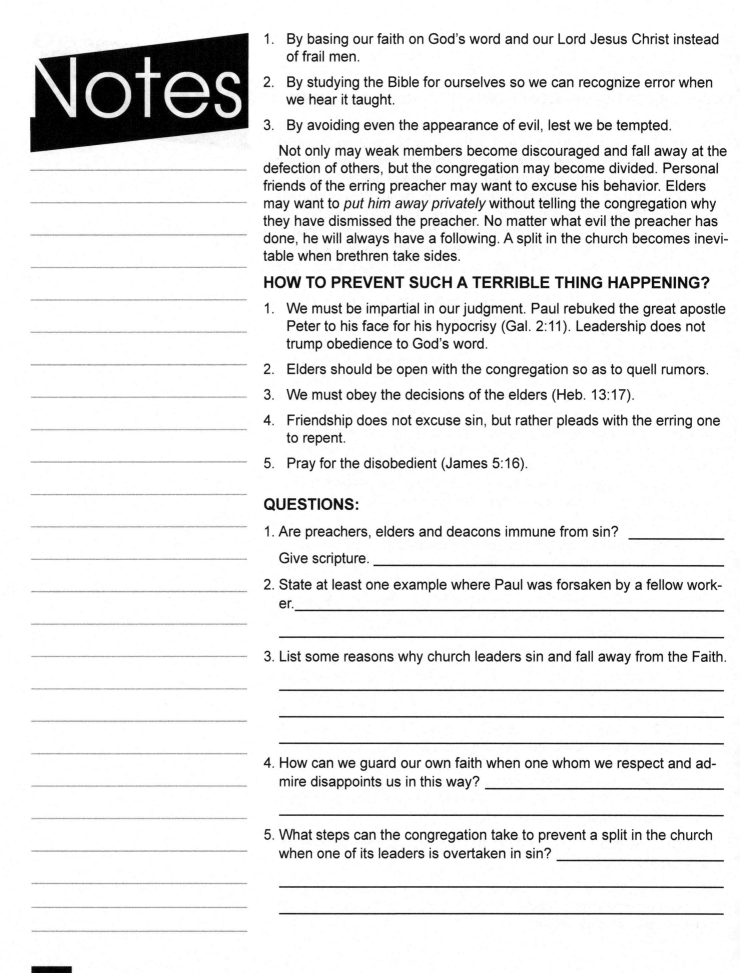

1. By basing our faith on God's word and our Lord Jesus Christ instead of frail men.

2. By studying the Bible for ourselves so we can recognize error when we hear it taught.

3. By avoiding even the appearance of evil, lest we be tempted.

Not only may weak members become discouraged and fall away at the defection of others, but the congregation may become divided. Personal friends of the erring preacher may want to excuse his behavior. Elders may want to *put him away privately* without telling the congregation why they have dismissed the preacher. No matter what evil the preacher has done, he will always have a following. A split in the church becomes inevitable when brethren take sides.

HOW TO PREVENT SUCH A TERRIBLE THING HAPPENING?

1. We must be impartial in our judgment. Paul rebuked the great apostle Peter to his face for his hypocrisy (Gal. 2:11). Leadership does not trump obedience to God's word.

2. Elders should be open with the congregation so as to quell rumors.

3. We must obey the decisions of the elders (Heb. 13:17).

4. Friendship does not excuse sin, but rather pleads with the erring one to repent.

5. Pray for the disobedient (James 5:16).

QUESTIONS:

1. Are preachers, elders and deacons immune from sin? _____

   Give scripture. _____

2. State at least one example where Paul was forsaken by a fellow worker._____

   _____

3. List some reasons why church leaders sin and fall away from the Faith.

   _____

   _____

   _____

4. How can we guard our own faith when one whom we respect and admire disappoints us in this way? _____

   _____

5. What steps can the congregation take to prevent a split in the church when one of its leaders is overtaken in sin? _____

   _____

   _____

Church Troubles (2):

DIVISIONS IN THE CHURCH

How important is unity in the church? By our actions, it would seem that unity among brethren is something that would be nice to have but not very realistic to expect. In some congregations, business meetings have ended in fisticuffs over differences of opinion. I have been in congregations where a business meeting was the signal for the men to bring up all the stored up grievances against brethren since the last meeting. Churches have split over personality clashes, family feuds, offenses in regard to church discipline, failure on the part of brethren to submit themselves to the elders (1 Pet. 5:5), a lack of communication between the elders and the brethren, matters of judgment and lack of humility in wanting the preeminence in the church (remember Diotrephes in 3 John 9).

Do we really believe that church unity is optional?

CHRIST'S PLEA FOR UNITY

Shortly before our Lord's betrayal, as He was giving a farewell message to His disciples, Jesus lifted up His eyes to heaven and prayed fervently that His disciples would be united in love and united in God and Christ. Listen to the words of Jesus in John 17:18-21: *"As You sent Me into the world, I also have sent them into the world. For their sakes I sanctify Myself, that they themselves also may be sanctified in truth. I do not ask on behalf of these alone, but for those also who believe in Me through their word; that they may all be one; even as You, Father, are in Me and I in You, that they also may be in Us, so that the world may believe that You sent Me."*

Notice the reason Jesus made such an impassioned prayer – *". . . **that the world may believe that You sent Me.**"* Divisions among God's people drive non-Christians away. They dissuade non-believers from a faith in Christ as the Son of God. Who in his right mind would want to be a part of a quarrelsome group of church goers who can't get along? Is this what is meant by letting our light shine in a world of darkness (Matt. 5:16)?

Paul makes the same plea to the quarreling Corinthians – *"Now I exhort you, brethren, by the name of our Lord Jesus Christ, that you all agree and that there be no divisions among you, but that you be made complete in the same mind and in the same judgment"* (1 Cor. 1:10).

HOW CAN UNITY BE ACCOMPLISHED?

It is the will of God and Christ that His people be of

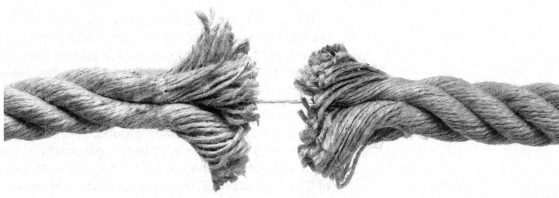

the same mind and the same judgment. How is this to be accomplished in view of the church being composed of people from all walks of life, all nationalities, and often very diverse backgrounds? Paul gives part of the answer in Ephesians 4:1-3, *"Therefore I, the prisoner of the Lord, implore you to walk in a manner worthy of the calling with which you have been called, with all humility and gentleness, with patience, showing tolerance for one another in love, being diligent to preserve the unity of the Spirit in the bond of peace."*

1. **PATIENCE**. We must exercise patience with one another. That includes patience with the new Christian with limited knowledge and much to learn. It includes patience with the weak brother trying to overcome sin.

2. **TOLERANCE.** We must exercise tolerance with those of different opinions and backgrounds, those who are slow to learn, and those who come up with seemingly off-the-wall statements. This does not mean we should ever tolerate sins unrepented of, teachers of error, or those who cause dissension (Rom. 16:17).

3. **LOVE**. *"So, as those who have been chosen of God, holy and beloved, put on a heart of compassion, kindness, humility, gentleness and patience; bearing with one another, and forgiving each other, whoever has a complaint against anyone; just as the Lord forgave you, so also should you. Beyond all these things put on love, which is the perfect bond of unity. Let the peace of Christ rule in your hearts, to which indeed you were called in one body; and be thankful"* (Col. 3:12-15). Love, kindness, humility, gentleness, and patience will enable us to work and worship together in harmony. We will seek the other's good and not our own. We will try to see the other's viewpoint. We will never display the attitude of *"My way"* or *"No way."* We will strive to develop a forgiving nature.

WHEN DIVISIONS COME

Our faith is not in men. *"So that your faith would not rest on the wisdom of men, but on the power of God"* (1 Cor. 2:5). Men will disappoint us. Men will betray our confidence in them. Men will fail us. It should come as no surprise since we are all frail and fallible beings. Our faith *must* be built on Christ and His word. The Lord is our hope; not some preacher – no matter how well spoken or how well educated; not the person who introduced us to the Gospel; not our closest friend; not the building the church meets in. A division in the church should not weaken our faith or cause us to fall away, though it will certainly make us heart sore.

Regardless of how others speak and act, and things can get pretty ugly, we must be sure we speak and act in a Christlike manner. We must keep a level head and not get swept up in partisan wranglings. Paul admonished the Corinthians against this when he was aware they were lining up behind various men and becoming followers of men rather than of Christ.

When doctrinal issues are involved, we must take a firm stand for the truth, even if it means standing alone. There is never a reason to join ourselves to a denomination or to a group who is practicing error, no matter how much love they profess. True love is to keep the commandments of Christ (1 John 5:3). How can one who has known the truth and tasted of the true fellowship of Christians go back into the world of darkness and error?

Do admonish our erring brethren with a sincere love for their souls. Pray for the love demonstrated in 1 Corinthians 13.

If I speak with the tongues of men and of angels, but do not have love, I have become a noisy gong or a clanging cymbal. If I have the gift of prophecy, and know all mysteries and all knowledge; and if I have all faith, so as to remove mountains, but do not have love, I am nothing. And if I give all my possessions to feed the poor, and if I surrender my body to be burned, but do not have love, it profits me nothing. Love is patient, love is kind and is not jealous; love does not brag and is not arrogant, does not act unbecomingly; it does not seek its own, is not provoked, does not take into account a wrong suffered, does not rejoice in unrighteousness, but rejoices with the truth; bears all things, believes all things, hopes all things, endures all things. Love never fails; but if there are gifts of prophecy, they will be done away; if there are tongues, they will cease; if there is knowledge, it will be done away. For we know in part and we prophesy in part; but when the perfect comes, the partial will be done away. When I was a child, I used to speak like a child, think like a child, reason like a child; when I became a man, I did away with childish things. For now we see in a mirror dimly, but then face to face; now I know in part, but then I will know fully just as I also have been fully known. But now faith, hope, love, abide these three; but the greatest of these is love.

LOVE IS
- Patient
- Kind
- Rejoices with the Truth
- Bears all things
- Believes all things
- Hopes all things
- Endures all things
- Never failing

LOVE IS NOT
- Jealous
- Boastful
- Arrogant
- Does not act unbecomingly
- Does not seek its own
- Provoked
- Does not take into account a wrong suffered
- Does not rejoice in unrighteousness

An idle church soon becomes a quarreling church. If we are not busy growing spiritually ourselves, bringing the Good News to our neighbors and the community, and looking after each other's needs, we soon spend our time looking inward, finding fault with each other and meddling into each other's affairs. We must strive wholeheartedly to love one another, love the souls of the lost enough to be busy teaching them Christ's Way of salvation and training up our children to become the next generation of workers in the church. Only then will we have the unity our Savior so earnestly prayed for!

Notes

Notes

_____

_____

_____

_____

_____

_____

_____

_____

_____

_____

_____

_____

_____

_____

_____

_____

_____

_____

_____

QUESTIONS:

1. Find as many scriptures as you can to show the importance of unity in the church._____

_____

_____

2. What reason did Christ give for Christians to be united? _____

_____

_____

3. In your experience, what are the main causes of dissension and division in the church? _____

_____

_____

4. What steps can a congregation take to ensure unity prevails and division is prevented? _____

_____

5. What can you do to become part of the solution to church problems and avoid becoming part of the problems? _____

_____

_____

On The Road Again

MOVING AWAY FROM FAMILY & FRIENDS

Being women and nesters by virtue of our femininity, it is natural that we would want to settle down near parents and kin folks and raise our families, who would then in turn build their nests nearby. Is that such a wrong desire? Not at all. With parents nearby, we can turn to them for advice and counsel and be there to help as age renders them feeble and unable to do many things for themselves. In like manner, with our children and their families nearby, we can render that same counsel to them as they in turn take over chores for us as our bodies age. In fact, the Bible teaches us to honor our parents in this way and to guide and instruct those women younger than we.

At the same time, however, we are taught not to love this present world nor to place family relationships before our service to God. *"He who loves father or mother more than Me is not worthy of Me. And he who loves son or daughter more than Me is not worthy of Me"* (Matt. 10:37).

But life doesn't always turn out that way, does it? As the saying goes, "Man proposes but God disposes." In the first century, Christians were scattered because of persecution (Acts 8:1-3).

Many left houses, lands, and even families for the gospel's sake. *"And everyone who has left houses or brothers or sisters or father or mother or children or farms for My name's sake, will receive many times as much, and will inherit eternal life"* (Matt. 19:29).

"Peter, an apostle of Jesus Christ, to those who reside as aliens, scattered throughout Pontus, Galatia, Cappadocia, Asia, and Bithynia" (1 Pet. 1:1).

Consider some of the reasons we may have to uproot our nest in one place and begin again in another:

- Preacher's family
- Military family
- Diplomatic service
- Corporate moves
- Lack of jobs in present area
- Education
- Athletic coach's family
- Political service
- Husband's wanderlust or love of adventure
- Political and/or religious persecution – asylum seekers

Do we have the right to refuse to move with our husbands? God, in His infinite wisdom, gave the headship of the family to the husband. *"For the husband is the head of the wife, as Christ also is the head of the church, He Himself being the Savior of the body. But as the church is subject to Christ, so also the wives ought to be to*

Notes

their husbands in everything" (Eph. 5:23). He, therefore, has the final say. We may present our reasons for not wanting to move, such as

* No sound church in the new location
* The children's education
* Needed by family
* Just plain don't want to move

As one who has moved approximately fifty times both across the country and overseas, believe me, I have used all the arguments at one time or another. Moving is never easy. You may get to be an expert at packing up and setting up your household in a new location, but it doesn't get any easier, especially emotionally. With the right attitude, however, and with God's help, we can do it! Don't forget: *This is your life.* Make every moment count! Don't make the mistake of thinking you will put your life on hold until you can move back *home.* I have made it a practice to hang one picture on the wall before going to bed the first night in our new home. That way it immediately becomes *our* home.

TRAVEL
"Travel broadens one," they say.
To which I add a hearty, "Aye,
It broadens one in every way:"

From my cosy, friendly, little world
Of a sudden I am hurled
Into a far-off, strange, new world.

Into a land of many races
Filled with seas of unknown faces
And quite unpronounceable places.

Where unfamiliar sights and sounds
Crowd in upon me and surround,
Amaze, delight, bewilder, and confound.

Until that day of jubilation
When, no longer filled with trepidation,
I find my place in this new nation!

The babble of voices becomes more than a noise
Their swift understanding brings pleasure and poise
And friendships and laughter and countless more joys.

Oh, travel does broaden one's circle of friends
And enlarges one's heart so your love has no end,
'Tho' the frequent departings to the marrow will rend.
                                        —Betty Tope

No matter how many arguments we make, in the end, it is the husband who must make the final decision as head of the house and we must learn to graciously abide by it. We do not have the option of refusing to go. Consider the example of Sarah who followed Abraham from the land of their birth in the Ur of the Chaldees to an unknown land, living in tents during the journey. We are told that Ur was a very modern and beautiful city with running water, tiled baths, beautiful temples, exquisite china and crystal, beautiful art work and jewelry. It could not have been easy to leave all this luxury and set out for the unknown on a perpetual camping trip!

Neither should we have the attitude of "*I told you so,*" when things do not work out as planned. No one is perfect and no one has perfect wisdom. Mistakes will be made, but as a loving help meet to our husbands, we must make the best of every situation.

Life is an adventure . . . we can make it a joyful one or one of misery. Determine ahead of time that you will be happy in your new home. Instead of dwelling on the friends and amenities you left behind, make new friends and seek out new activities to enjoy. If there is an established congregation of the Lord's people, get acquainted with as many members as you can. Invite families into your home or call on them in theirs. Don't sit at home feeling sorry for yourself because you don't know anyone. Take an active part in the worship and work of the church. Volunteer to teach a class, prepare the communion, clean the building, etc. Your cheerful attitude and willingness to work will endear yourself to all.

If there is no sound congregation available, begin worshiping in your home and invite others to join you. Use every opportunity to teach the gospel to your new neighbors, the people you meet on a daily basis in town. Join the garden club or some other organization so you can meet new friends and prospects. You will grow spiritually as you learn to depend more on the Lord and less on family and friends left behind. As you study to teach your new neighbors and friends, you will find your Bible knowledge increasing proportionately.

Every place has its own beauty if we but seek it. Take time to explore the highways and the byways of your new surroundings. Visit local historical sites and read up on the local history. Take advantage of new foods, new culture, new climate, and its resulting activities. Use this opportunity for personal growth.

You will be the richer for every sacrifice you have made. God blesses us abundantly when we joyfully do His will.

Remember the beautiful words of Ruth as Naomi was about to depart Moab and return to her own land:

> *"Do not urge me to leave you*
> *or turn back from following you;*
> *for where you go, I will go,*
> *and where you lodge, I will lodge.*
> *Your people shall be my people,*
> *and your God, my God.*
> *Where you die, I will die,*
> *and there I will be buried.*
> *Thus may the LORD do to me, and worse,*
> *if anything but death parts you and me"* (Ruth 1:16-17).

Notes

QUESTIONS:

1. Why might it become necessary to move away from family and friends?

_____

_____

_____

2. What are some excuses we are prone to give for not wanting to make the move? _____

_____

_____

_____

3. To whom has God given the ultimate decision? Give scripture. _____

_____

_____

4. Do we have the right to refuse to move with our husbands? Give scripture. _____

_____

_____

5. What are some things we can do to insure our happiness in our new location? _____

_____

_____

Financial Difficulties

We live in an age of great economic turmoil. Factories and businesses that have been in operation for generations are going out of business. Whole cities are deserted and dying as manufacturing jobs disappear from the areas. We are shocked and saddened when we see pictures of these once thriving communities now boarded up, derelict, and empty. Closer to home we anguish over the plight of brethren and family members who have lost jobs and in many instances their life-time savings and homes. We ourselves may become victims of our times.

Throughout history there have been times of prosperity and times of poverty. Famine, earthquakes, fires, floods, wars, and economic downturns have caused people not only to suffer reverses in their financial situations, but many have lost all. In New Testament times Christians often gave up jobs, homes, lands, and even families through persecution. *"And on that day a great persecution began against the church in Jerusalem, and they were all scattered throughout the regions of Judea and Samaria, except the apostles"* (Acts 8:1b).

During World War II the Jewish population in Nazi Germany and occupied countries saw their homes and possessions taken away from them, leaving them destitute. During the Great Depression in this country, there was mass migration as men walked the roads and hitched rides in railroad cars searching for jobs anywhere they could find them. During this time, my husband's family lived by the railroad track in a western town and my mother-in-law has told us many times that hardly a day went by during those years that some needy man didn't knock on her door asking for food. She never turned any of them away, even though she was hard pressed to feed her own family of six growing boys.

WHAT ARE SOME OF THE EFFECTS ON AN INDIVIDUAL WHO IS OUT OF WORK?

It doesn't take very many rejections by potential employers for the job-seeker to begin to suffer from low self esteem. He may lose whatever self confidence in his abilities he once had. It matters not why a person is passed over for somebody else. All he can see is that he is unqualified, unworthy, and unwanted. The longer a person is out of work, the

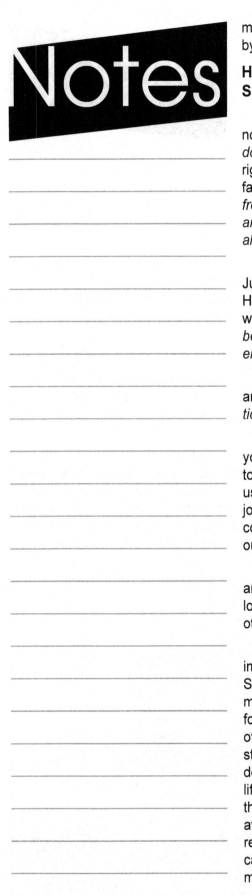

more intensified these feelings become. Depression may set in, followed by despondency and an abandonment of hope.

HOW ARE WE TO HANDLE OURSELVES IN THESE SITUATIONS AND BE PLEASING TO GOD?

Over and over in God's word we are instructed to trust in God and not riches. David in Psalm 62:10b instructs us thusly, *"If riches increase, do not set your heart upon them."* Riches can be fleeting. Consider the righteous, rich man Job. In one day he lost all his possessions and all his family except his wife. His answer to this great calamity: *"'Naked I came from my mother's womb, and naked I shall return there. The Lord gave and the Lord has taken away, blessed be the name of the Lord.' Through all this Job did not sin nor did he blame God"* (Job 1:21, 22).

Moreover, we are instructed by Jesus, in Matthew 6:25-34, not to worry. Just as God takes care of the birds of the air and the lilies of the field, so He will take care of us. He knows our needs. We must exercise patience, wait on the Lord, and not borrow trouble for the morrow. *"Therefore do not be anxious for tomorrow, for tomorrow will care for itself. Each day has enough trouble of its own"* (Matt. 6:34, NASV).

Rather than spending our time in hand wringing, Paul says in Philippians 4:6, *"Be anxious for nothing, but in everything by prayer and supplication with thanksgiving let your requests be made known to God."*

Be diligent in your job search. All the experts I have read after say you should spend as many hours a day looking for work as you expect to spend once on the job. Network. Be willing to take a job out of your usual field. Be willing to take less money than you were making on the old job. Consider temp work. Sometimes just getting a foot in the door of a company will lead to full-time work with better pay. Try to keep a positive outlook and don't give up!

Don't let pride get in the way of allowing others to help. Our brethren are usually quick to offer help on a temporary basis with bills you can no longer meet. But they are not mind readers. When you have exhausted all other avenues, do let your brethren know that you need help.

Economize! If you are laid off, retrenched, etc., begin to economize immediately. Stop eating out! Stop picking up fast food to bring home! Stop buying packaged meals! Learn to cook. You can prepare delicious meals from scratch at a fraction of the cost of pre-cooked or packaged foods. Start packing lunches for children and spouses. If necessary, cut off the cable or satellite TV. These are luxury items, not necessities. Our standard of living in this country is so high that we have become dependent upon many luxuries that we can easily give up and still have a good life. This is a good opportunity to once again enjoy a level of family time that we may have forgotten. Explain to the children that you can no longer afford all the extra-curricular activities they are involved in. Children are resilient and will understand once the situation is explained to them. You can even enlist their help in suggesting more ways the family can economize. They will rise to the challenge!

HOW CAN WE HELP OTHERS IN THIS SITUATION?

Be sympathetic to the needs of others. Pray for them and let them know you are praying. Don't be like an elder I know of who, when asked to pray for her out-of-work husband, told the young wife and mother that he didn't have time to pray for her husband and their family. If we are too busy to pray for our suffering brothers and sisters, we are too busy!

Be on the lookout for possible job openings for your brother or sister. Check your newspaper want ads. Be alert to advertisements on TV. Check the job listings at your place of work.

Offer to help them financially or any other way necessary. They may need help with bills, could use a grocery gift card, transportation to a job interview, or even the offer of a temporary home.

Right after the tragedy of 9/11 our very distressed financial advisor telephoned me. He had the unpleasant task of phoning all his clients to give them some sort of assurance that all was not lost. I could tell he had already dealt with many irate and worried clients that day. I found myself reassuring him that he needn't worry about us. We knew we were in God's hands. If we were to lose all our savings due to this invasion of our country, we would manage. I told him our parents had lived through the Great Depression and so would we. We had no idea what the future held for any of us financially or otherwise. We weathered that storm and now are facing another one with the specter of financial collapse around the world. We cannot waste our time worrying over things beyond our control. We *can* do all in our power to help ourselves. We *can* tighten our belts personally, live within our means and save for hard times to come. We *can* send a message to our congressmen to do the same. We *can* cast all our cares upon our loving heavenly Father and trust in Him to do for us that which we cannot do for ourselves. We *can* have the peace of God which passeth all understanding even in uncertain times like these.

Finally, Paul has this instruction: *"Instruct those who are rich in this present world not to be conceited or to fix their hope on the uncertainty of riches, but on God, who richly supplies us with all things to enjoy. Instruct them to do good, to be rich in good works, to be generous and ready to share, storing up for themselves the treasure of a good foundation for the future, so that they may take hold of that which is life indeed"* (1 Tim. 6:17-19).

Notes

QUESTIONS:

1. Why did many first-century Christians lose possessions, houses, and lands? _____

   _____

2. Give one or more scriptures against worry. _____

   _____

3. Give some practical suggestions for the job seeker. _____

   _____

   _____

4. What are some ways we can economize? _____

   _____

   _____

5. What are some ways you can help the brother or sister who is out of work? _____

   _____

Civil and Political Upheaval

For by Him all things were created,both in the heavens and on earth, visible and invisible, whether thrones or dominions or rulers or authorities – all things have been created through Him and for Him (Col. 1:16).

Throughout history the world has experienced times of peace and prosperity and times of political upheaval, persecution, and even war.

Today is no exception. As I write this, our country is at war on two fronts. Christians are facing more and more persecution, even in our own country. The political scene is viewed by the majority as another battle front. Many of our citizens remind me of Chicken Little who, after being hit on the head by an acorn, went around yelling, "The sky is falling down, the sky is falling down." We see worry, confusion, fear, and even despondency on every hand. Besides all this, some would have us feel guilty that we as individuals are bringing about the destruction of the earth simply by living.

Yet, the Christian can have peace even in tumultuous times like these. We have the assurance that God is in control. *"Let the name of God be blessed forever and ever, for wisdom and power belong to Him. It is He who changes the times and epochs; He removes kings and establishes kings: He gives wisdom to wise men and knowledge to men of understanding. It is He who reveals the profound and hidden things: and the light dwells with Him. To You, O God of my fathers, I give thanks and praise, even now You have made known to me what we requested of You"* (Dan. 2:20-23).

Nothing in this world happens without God's knowledge. He has the power to remove kings and establish kings. It is God who changes the times and epochs of humanity. Sometimes He allows brutal dictators to reign over countries to bring about His will. Think of all the examples in the Old Testament when God allowed the enemies of Israel to overrun them in order to bring them back to Him, and then helped the Israelites to overturn their enemies when the people repented. Throughout the time of the Judges, God would raise up a judge to defeat their enemies as the people cried to God for help. Once peace and prosperity were returned to the land, the people would become complacent, forget about God, and return to their idolatry. So the cycle would begin again.

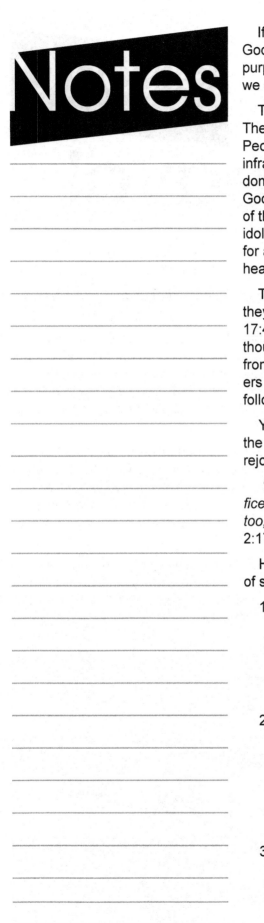

If we as a nation suffer war and persecution, it is to fulfill a purpose of God. If we as Christians suffer persecution, it is also meant to serve His purpose. We may not always understand the reason for our suffering, but we can take heart in knowing God has a purpose and He is in control.

The church was not established during times of peace and tranquility. The mighty Roman Empire ruled its far-flung subjects with a rod of iron. People were enslaved, imprisoned, and often brutally put to death for their infractions of Roman law. Idolatry and immorality were rife. Human wisdom would have chosen a more auspicious time for the birth of the Son of God and the establishing of His Kingdom. But God knew better! In spite of the horrific persecution, and the hatred of Christianity by the immoral idolaters, people were longing for something better. They were longing for a better life, longing for peace, longing for the hope of heaven. The heavier the persecution, the more the church grew!

The political and religious leaders of the day feared the church because they viewed it as a danger to their positions of leadership and power (Acts 17:4, 5). Just as the silversmiths of Ephesus were in an uproar over the thought of losing their trade and their livelihood when the people turned from idolatry to Christianity (Acts 19:23-41), so the immoral political leaders of today fear the teachings of Christ, knowing if enough citizens truly follow Christ, their own livelihoods would be in jeopardy.

Yet, in the midst of an idolatrous, immoral, and often corrupt society, the Christians of Philippi were admonished by Paul time and time again to rejoice!

"But even if I am being poured out as a drink offering upon the sacrifice and service of your faith, I rejoice and share my joy with you all. You too, I urge you, rejoice in the same way and share your joy with me" (Phil. 2:17, 18). *"Rejoice in the Lord always; again I will say, rejoice!"* (Phil. 4:4).

How were the Christians in Philippi to accomplish this joy in the midst of such turmoil?

1. They were admonished to **stand fast.** *"Therefore, my beloved brethren whom I long to see, my joy and crown, so stand firm in the Lord, my beloved"* (Phil. 4:1, NASV). In other words, don't let the trials and uncertainties of the present age to frighten and discourage you from reaching your eternal goal. Even the devil will flee if we stand fast and confront him (James 4:7).

2. They were instructed to **live in harmony.** *"I urge Euodia and I urge Syntyche to live in harmony in the Lord. Indeed, true comrade, I ask you also to help these women, who have shared my struggle in the cause of the gospel, together with Clement also, and the rest of my fellow workers, whose names are in the book of life"* (Phil. 4:2-3, NASV). Discord within the church brings derision from the world and causes some within to become disheartened and fall away.

3. They were instructed to **pray.** *"Be anxious for nothing, but in everything by prayer and supplication with thanksgiving let your requests be made known to God. And the peace of God, which surpasses all comprehension, shall guard your hearts and your minds in Christ Jesus"* (Phil. 4:6, NASV). Prayer in faith brings peace and tranquil-

ity. No matter how bad the news of the day, we can lay down our heads at night in peace, knowing our God is in charge. Truly, the peace of God surpasses all comprehension and it will guard our hearts and our minds in Christ Jesus. How can we worry and fret *the sky is falling down* when we have turned our worries, fears, angers, hurts, disappointments, and concerns over to our all-loving, all-knowing, all-seeing, all-powerful God in heaven?

4. Finally, our Philippian brethren were commanded to have **right thinking.** *"Finally, brethren, whatever is true, whatever is honorable, whatever is right, whatever is pure, whatever is lovely, whatever is of good repute, if there is any excellence and if anything worthy of praise, let your mind dwell on these things"* (Phil. 4:8). We do have power over what we think! We are in control of our thoughts. If the daily news upsets us, turn off the radio and TV or turn them to soothing music. If we are traveling in the car, we can sing hymns that will lift our spirits and remind us of God's love and power. If the reading of the daily newspaper depresses us, cancel the subscription and take a walk outside instead. There is nothing like observing the beauties of nature to restore one's soul.

We are but wayfarers and pilgrims passing through this world, which is but a temporary home for us. Our true home is in heaven. When we remember that, we will not be too concerned about whatever dire thing is happening in our world.

"For our citizenship is in heaven, from which also we eagerly wait for a Savior, the Lord Jesus Christ; who will transform the body of our humble state into conformity with the body of His glory, by the exertion of the power that He has even to subject all things to Himself" (Phil. 3:20, 21).

QUESTIONS:

1. Are the turmoils in the world today something new? _____ Give examples of God's people who lived under hostile governments or through natural disasters. _____

_____

_____

2. Who is in control of governments? Give scripture to prove your answer and one example. _____

3. What was the political and civil climate like in Jerusalem when the church was established? _____

_____

4. List four ways we can have peace and joy regardless of what is happening around us. _____

_____

_____

_____

5. Where is our true home? _____

Notes

lesson 10

Loss of Health

Sometimes life throws you a curve when you least expect it. You can be busily going about your daily affairs, caring for family and home and trying to the best of your abilities to serve God in all the other ways His Word directs, when you are struck with a life-changing illness. It may start out slowly with nothing more than flu symptoms. But then, as the days and weeks pass, those symptoms don't go away. In fact, they not only do not go away, but they get worse. The tiredness becomes fatigue so severe you can't even hold a book to read. The aches become actual pain from your head to your toes. You eventually have to quit going grocery shopping because the pain in your ankles feels like a million little broken bones. You are worn out just walking from the car to the store entrance. The fatigue prevents you from every kind of housework, so you feel guilty doing nothing while your husband and friends take over your responsibilities. You notice an increased sensitivity to light and noise. Your thought processes are so messed up you can't think straight. You may call this fog brain, cheese brain, or just fuzzy headedness. After years of touch typing you discover your brain transposes letters and leaves entire words out of sentences.

Doctors begin using words like Chronic Fatigue and Fibromyalgia. They send you to a round of specialists to rule out other scary auto-immune diseases and in the end you may get the official verdict: Connective Tissue Disorder, Chronic Fatigue Syndrome, Myofacial Pain Disorder and Severe Fibromyalgia. (Substitute your own life-changing diagnosis here such as Lupus, MS, Crohn's disease, Rheumatoid Arthritis, etc., or permanent injury from an accident.) Next, you learn there is no cure.

How do we handle news like this?

The apostle Paul has this to say about his own infirmity:

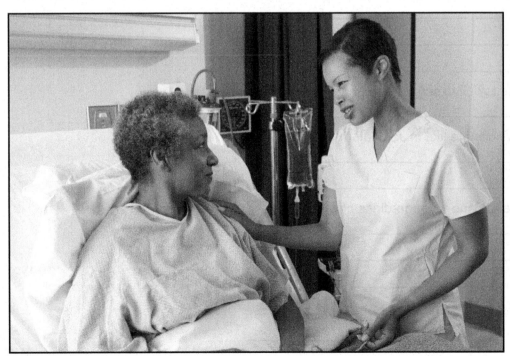

And lest I should be exalted above measure through the abundance of the revelations, there was given to me a thorn in the flesh, the messenger of Satan to buffet me, lest I should be exalted above measure. For this thing I besought the Lord thrice, that it might depart from me. And he said unto me, My grace is sufficient for thee: for my strength is made perfect in weakness. Most gladly therefore will I rather glory in my infirmities, that the power of Christ may rest upon me (2 Cor. 12:7-9, KJV).

Most of us will not immediately *gladly glory* in our infirmities. Most likely we will go through the same or similar steps of mourning and grief one goes through over the death of a loved one. For, a death *has* occurred . . . the death of our former self. We will never again be the energetic, healthy persons we once were. Somehow, we must learn to live with this new self and learn to be happy and praise God for the abilities we *do* have.

You may learn the medical profession in general has little to offer other than drugs to mask your pain, the side effects of which may be worse than the original problem. So, you learn to research everything you can find on the subject. You may join a support group of friends similarly afflicted, a community support group, or even the national one. You will find varied forms of advice offered and soon realize what helps one may not help another. Some find diet, exercise when able, and rest, rest, rest are most effective along with a number of supplements.

Massages help some and aggravate others. The same goes with Chiropractic treatment. Some find it extremely helpful but it makes others worse. Most doctors will tell you to learn to live within your envelope. In other words, know your limitations. You do this by trial and error. Some activities you will find you can't do at all and others are okay in moderation. Usually you don't realize your limits until you've crossed the line. Another problem is that of overextending yourself on a rare "good" day. You are so happy to be active and productive again that you almost always do too much and then are disabled again while you recover.

Then comes the realization: *This is my life.* This condition is not going to go away but we still have obligations to God, the church, and our family. Taking care of ourselves must be a priority so we can do the other things God expects of us. We must make time for study of God's word and prayer. We must learn to say "no" to some things and not try to be heroic. We may have to learn to be a party-pooper and get to bed on time, realizing we must have nine hours of sleep to function when others may get by on six.

Instead of focusing on what we *can't* do, we must now focus on what we *can* do. We may not be able to show hospitality by cooking meals for guests but we can occasionally take a family out to eat. We may not be able to handle the stress of teaching a children's class, but we can look for other ways to serve by sending cards to visitors, shut-ins, the sick, and by making encouraging phone calls. Usually, we won't hurt any more by being at worship than we will by staying home. We learn to put on a smile and a brightly-colored dress and go on. We learn to gloss over the question, "How are you today?" with something like, "I'm so happy to see you," or "I'm glad to be here today." We certainly don't want to tell 80 to 100 people that we are feeling terrible!

Here are some practical ideas for coping with the changes in your life:

- If you can't hold your Bible, listen to it on tape, CD, Ipod, etc.

- Listen to hymns and sermons at home if you are unable to assemble with the saints. Many congregations have web sites that allow you to listen to the sermons.

- If you can't remember or focus on long passages, write out a verse on an index card and think on that verse for the day or week.

Notes

Notes

- Keep a journal of things you can do or have accomplished, even if it was to pray for others. You will soon see that there are things you can do even from bed.

- Keep a journal of kindnesses shown to you or a shoe box with cards or things that make you smile.

- If you are a mother of little ones, listen to books on tape together or have them read to you while you snuggle on the bed. Have them help you make cards to send to others.

- Don't be too proud or independent to accept help from others when offered.

If we had not known pain, we could not have the same compassion for others dealing with painful conditions. If we had not known this awful fatigue, we might not have learned to rely on God for our strength. We may still suffer from guilt over not being able to do all the former acts of service we used to do, but we should keep reminding ourselves that God knows our limitations and does not require more of us than we are able. However, we must not deceive ourselves into thinking we can do nothing. We must continually strive to come to the realization that whatever life hands us in the way of physical infirmities, God's grace is sufficient to see us through and Heaven awaits us after death where there is no night, no pain, and no sorrow.

QUESTIONS:

1. What was Paul's reaction to infirmity (2 Cor. 12:7-9)? _____

_____

_____

2. What lessons can we learn from Paul in how he handled his infirmities?

_____

_____

_____

3. "Joy" or "rejoice" is mentioned eighteen times in the book of Philippians. Contrast this with Paul's mention of his infirmity. What lesson can we draw from this? _____

_____

_____

4. List some typical reactions upon learning one has an incurable illness.

_____

_____

_____

5. Name some blessings associated with a chronic illness. _____

_____

_____

Death of a Loved One

For what is your life? It is even a vapor that appears for a little time and then vanishes away (James 4:14b, NKJV).

If we live long enough, we will experience the loss of a loved one, be it father, mother, sibling, grandparent, husband, or some other relative or friend dear to us. No matter how old we are before the loss occurs, it is usually devastating. Even in the case of a prolonged illness where the outcome is obvious and certain, we are never quite ready to give up our loved one.

Long after her husband is gone, the widow may hold *conversations* with her husband. She may tell him about the problems she is having with her children, her finances, or any other overwhelming concern. Some get a great deal of comfort out of that.

With the loss of parents, there will come the urge to ask their advice at odd moments for many years. We long for what we no longer have – the security of being able to go to one who is wiser than we, who perhaps has trod the path we now find ourselves traversing.

Years after losing a child, we will find ourselves thinking of what that child would be like at this age, what accomplishments our child would have made, what our child would think of this or that situation, what he/she would be like as an adult.

At first, the grief will be overwhelming. We will usually find ourselves going through our daily routines by rote. We seem to tell ourselves if we don't think, we won't feel, and we will get through this day, this week, this month.

In time we will go through the seven stages of grief. They may not come in order and may be overlapping, but they will come. Remember, there is no set time to get through any of the stages.

1. **Shock and Denial**. This is the body's protection from being overwhelmed with grief before we can handle it.

2. **Pain and Guilt.** This is the time of unbelievable pain, but necessary if we are to eventually heal. It is a time

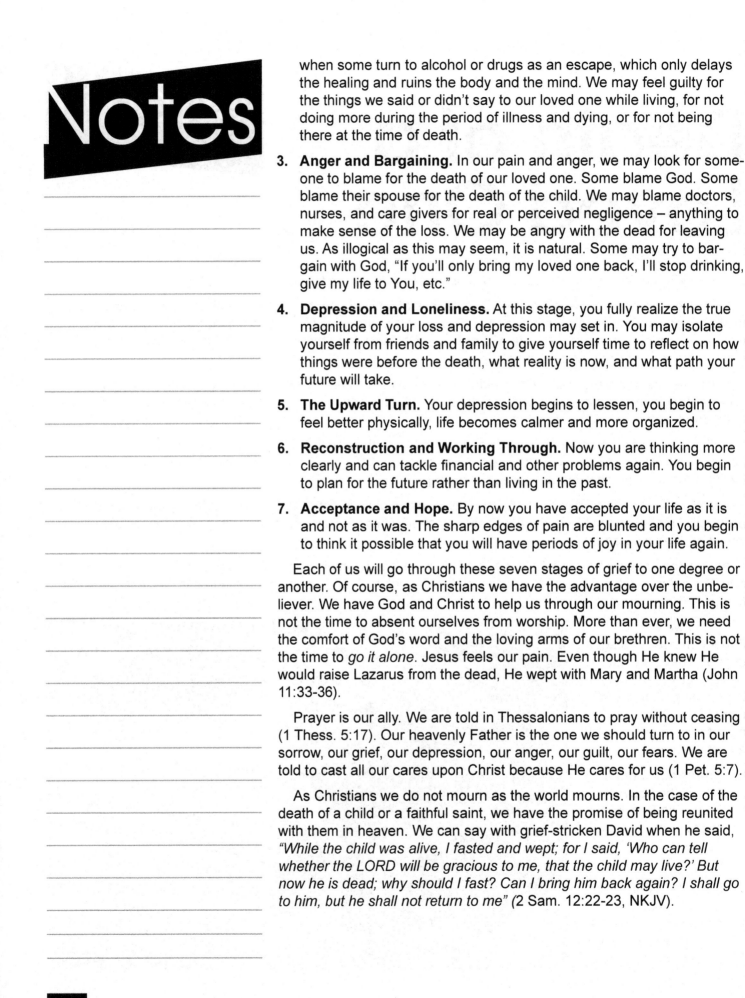

when some turn to alcohol or drugs as an escape, which only delays the healing and ruins the body and the mind. We may feel guilty for the things we said or didn't say to our loved one while living, for not doing more during the period of illness and dying, or for not being there at the time of death.

3. **Anger and Bargaining.** In our pain and anger, we may look for someone to blame for the death of our loved one. Some blame God. Some blame their spouse for the death of the child. We may blame doctors, nurses, and care givers for real or perceived negligence – anything to make sense of the loss. We may be angry with the dead for leaving us. As illogical as this may seem, it is natural. Some may try to bargain with God, "If you'll only bring my loved one back, I'll stop drinking, give my life to You, etc."

4. **Depression and Loneliness.** At this stage, you fully realize the true magnitude of your loss and depression may set in. You may isolate yourself from friends and family to give yourself time to reflect on how things were before the death, what reality is now, and what path your future will take.

5. **The Upward Turn.** Your depression begins to lessen, you begin to feel better physically, life becomes calmer and more organized.

6. **Reconstruction and Working Through.** Now you are thinking more clearly and can tackle financial and other problems again. You begin to plan for the future rather than living in the past.

7. **Acceptance and Hope.** By now you have accepted your life as it is and not as it was. The sharp edges of pain are blunted and you begin to think it possible that you will have periods of joy in your life again.

Each of us will go through these seven stages of grief to one degree or another. Of course, as Christians we have the advantage over the unbeliever. We have God and Christ to help us through our mourning. This is not the time to absent ourselves from worship. More than ever, we need the comfort of God's word and the loving arms of our brethren. This is not the time to *go it alone*. Jesus feels our pain. Even though He knew He would raise Lazarus from the dead, He wept with Mary and Martha (John 11:33-36).

Prayer is our ally. We are told in Thessalonians to pray without ceasing (1 Thess. 5:17). Our heavenly Father is the one we should turn to in our sorrow, our grief, our depression, our anger, our guilt, our fears. We are told to cast all our cares upon Christ because He cares for us (1 Pet. 5:7).

As Christians we do not mourn as the world mourns. In the case of the death of a child or a faithful saint, we have the promise of being reunited with them in heaven. We can say with grief-stricken David when he said, *"While the child was alive, I fasted and wept; for I said, 'Who can tell whether the LORD will be gracious to me, that the child may live?' But now he is dead; why should I fast? Can I bring him back again? I shall go to him, but he shall not return to me"* (2 Sam. 12:22-23, NKJV).

WHAT CAN WE DO FOR THOSE WHO HAVE LOST A LOVED ONE?

When we lost our precious five-year-old Karen, we were an ocean away from family. We could not afford a long-distance phone call and sent a telegram to our families with the sad news. But we were not bereft of comfort and consolation. Our South African brethren showered us with love and care. They provided food for all those who came to share our sorrow at her funeral. They cleaned our house. They stopped by to share a meal with us so we wouldn't have to look at the vacant chair at the kitchen table. They prayed with us. One family came from a distant city and stayed a week with us. Unknown brethren from back home wrote beautiful notes of consolation. Every gesture of love meant so much to us! Recently, a doctor asked me if I had gone for counseling when our daughter died. When I told her, no, she replied, "How did you ever get through it?" As Christians we get through our tragedies with the help of our brethren in Christ. Don't make the mistake of shutting your brethren out when you need them the most!

Some thoughtful acts of kindness are:
- Offer to make phone calls and take care of some of the myriad details that one in shock may overlook
- Clean house in preparation for the visitors
- Provide paper ware, not only for the visitation on the day of the funeral, but for several days or weeks after
- Offer to take the children to the park or some other happy place
- Offer to drive the grieved to their appointments
- Provide food and flowers
- Give plenty of hugs
- Talk with them about the good memories of their loved ones
- Give them space for their grieving when necessary
- Continue to keep in touch days and weeks later

I, personally, like the idea of making the funeral service or memorial a celebration of our loved one's life. Yes, it is a time for grief, but it is also a time for remembrances. Involve the younger family members in reciting a poem they have written about their grandfather, get a brother to recount some of the happy memories he has. My parents were not Christians and requested a direct cremation with no service upon their deaths. My sister and I honored their wishes, but I felt cheated. The one small paragraph of my father's death in the obituary column of the local newspaper offended me most of all. How can you reduce a person's life to one or two sentences? Where was the mention of his love of family, of fishing, of helping all his neighbors – whether in putting up storm windows and screens in Detroit or of shopping for the widows in his retirement mobile home park in Mesa? Where was the mention of the happy childhood he gave me? The work ethic he instilled in me and my sister?

> *Better to go to the house of mourning*
> *Than to go to the house of feasting,*
> *For that is the end of all men;*
> *And the living will take it to heart* (Eccl. 7:2, NKJV).

The wise man Solomon, said it is better to go to the house of mourning than to the house of feasting. Why? Because it makes us reflect on the fact that we all will die one day and face the judgment. The funeral service is a good opportunity to preach the Good News to those who should be in the frame of mind to think on spiritual things and reflect on whether they have prepared themselves for that day. How about you? Have you obeyed the Gospel of Jesus Christ so that you are ready for the final Judgment? Please read Acts 2:38, Mark 16:15-16, and Matthew 28:18-20.

QUESTIONS:

1. Discuss the seven stages of grief and how we can cope with them.

_____

_____

_____

_____

_____

_____

_____

_____

2. What can we do to help those who are grieving? _____

_____

_____

_____

3. How does God comfort us?_____

_____

4. Why does Solomon say it is better to go to a funeral than to a party?

_____

_____

_____

5. How can we prepare ourselves for Judgment Day? _____

_____

Widowhood

One of the most dreaded words in the English language is **"widow."** Whether we are young or old, we all dread the day the word "widow" applies to us.

Young wives and mothers are concerned about having to raise their children alone, a daunting enough task with both father and mother on hand, but overwhelming for a woman alone. She may be living far from family when she needs them the most. She will most likely have to look for work. If she has been out of the work force for a number of years, her skills may be outdated or nonexistent. I have one older friend who found herself in that position and the last job she had worked at was wrapping butter in a creamery. Not much call for that skill today! She not only lost her husband, she also lost her home as they were living in the preacher's home provided by the congregation. She had to downsize into a mobile home very quickly. I love and admire her so much for her graciousness in adversity. I never once heard her complain.

Older women are concerned about coping with dwindling finances, giving up their home, possibly having to move to another locality where their children can take care of them. This not only entails leaving a home she loves and no longer being able to extend hospitality to family and brethren, but also means leaving close friends and familiar doctors.

And all of these new hardships come at a time when a woman has lost her companion . . . her friend . . . her helper . . . her lover . . . her heart. In the beginning she is operating on auto pilot, doing tasks by rote, unthinking, maybe even unfeeling. Friends are usually there to help her get through the funeral and a few days afterwards. Gradually, they get back to their own lives. The widow suddenly faces an unknown future, adrift without the anchor of her husband. She must begin the grieving process while at the same time deal with the mountain of paper work a death entails. There may be medical bills and the paperwork associated with them that continue coming in for a year or longer. There are insurance papers, financial papers, Social Security, the IRS – the list seems endless.

We need to prepare ourselves now in the event the unthinkable happens. Statistics show one third of widows are under 65 years of age and 75 per cent of women 85 years and older are widows. Actuarial tables show men are far more apt to die before their wives. Nothing can prepare us for the grief and heartache of losing a husband, but we can take steps to minimize the shock of having to deal with all the paperwork. Some husbands genuinely want to spare their wives from financial worry in the day-to-day living, so they shield

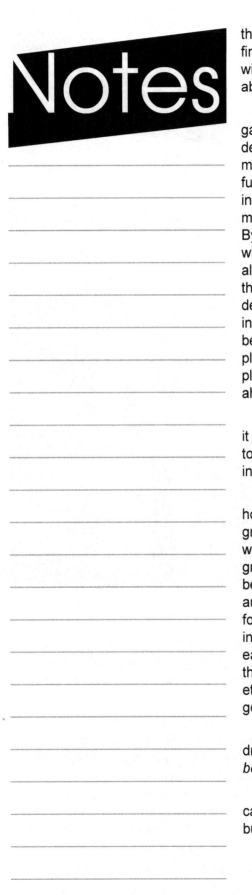

them from the bills, the taxes, the bank balance, and everything else of a financial nature. They are free to run the household and make purchases within the parameters he has set without worrying their pretty little heads about budgets and overdrafts.

That is totally unfair to the wife. She needs to know about the mortgage, the investments the family has, the car payments and credit card debts, any life insurance policies he may have taken out, pensions he may have coming to him, etc. If both husband and wife plan the financial future of the family together, it will be easier to make informed decisions in the event she is left a widow. All the experts say a widow should not make any major decisions for a year after the death of her husband. By then she will have a clearer picture of where she wants to live and what she wants to do with the rest of her life. This is good advice but not always possible to heed. As in the case of my friend who had to vacate the preacher's home when her preacher-husband died, sometimes big decisions have to be made fairly quickly. It may not be possible to stay in one's home and make the mortgage payments. The widow may not be able to take care of herself financially or physically. It helps to have a plan in place ahead of time. Just as governments and municipalities have plans in place for unforseen disasters, so we need to be wise and plan ahead ourselves.

Wise couples plan for their retirement. They try to figure out how much it will cost them to live when they retire, whether they want to move closer to their grown children, what kind of home they can afford and get around in, etc. Wise couples also plan for a surviving spouse.

Throughout the Old Testament God's people were given instructions on how they were to care for the fatherless and widows among them. In our grandparents' generation it was the norm for the children to care for their widowed mother or father. My uncle bought a little house for my widowed grandmother to live in and the siblings cared for her needs. When she became unable to live alone, she moved in with my uncle and aunt, my aunt being the eldest of the children. My grandmother had been widowed for about fifty years when she died. In her younger widowhood she took in washing and did sewing to care for her family. It was not unusual in the early 1900s for widows to establish boarding houses or restaurants in their homes to make ends meet. With the advent of Social Security, society more and more came to expect the elderly to care for themselves and go into nursing homes when they could no longer do so.

In 1 Timothy 5:14, Paul urges the young widows to marry and bear children and keep house: *"Therefore, I want younger widows to get married, bear children, keep house, and give the enemy no occasion for reproach."*

In the same passage, he admonishes children and grandchildren to care for their widowed mothers and grandmothers so the church won't be burdened.

Honor widows who are widows indeed; but if any widow has children or grandchildren, let them first learn to practice piety in regard to their own family, and to make some return to their parents; for this is acceptable in the sight of God. Now she who is a widow indeed, and who has been left alone has fixed her hope on God, and continues in entreaties and prayers night and day. But she who gives herself to wanton pleasure is dead even while she lives. Prescribe these things as well, so that they may be above reproach. But if anyone does not provide for his own, and especially for those of his household, he has denied the faith, and is worse than an unbeliever. Let a widow be put on the list only if she is not less than sixty years old, having been the wife of one man, having a reputation for good works; and if she has brought up children, if she has shown hospitality to strangers, if she has washed the saints' feet, if she has assisted those in distress, and if she has devoted herself to every good work. But refuse to put younger widows on the list, for when they feel sensual desires in disregard of Christ, they want to get married, thus incurring condemnation, because they have set aside their previous pledge. And at the same time they also learn to be idle, as they go around from house to house; and not merely idle, but also gossips and busybodies, talking about things not proper to mention. Therefore, I want younger widows to get married, bear children, keep house, and give the enemy no occasion for reproach; for some have already turned aside to follow Satan. If any woman who is a believer has dependent widows, let her assist them, and let not the church be burdened, so that it may assist those who are widows indeed (1 Tim. 5:3-16, NASV).

As Christians, we should strive throughout our lives to develop the attributes necessary for the widow to be cared for by the church in the absence of relatives. Apart from the age requirement, notice these:

- Having been the wife of one man
- Having a reputation for good works
- If she has brought up children
- If she has shown hospitality to strangers
- If she has washed the saints' feet
- If she has assisted those in distress
- If she has devoted herself to every good work

These spiritual preparations are the most important preparations we can make. Our ultimate dependence is upon God, our heavenly Father. He knows our hearts and minds, our cares, our worries, our sorrows. If we place our trust in Him, His promises and His word, we can survive anything, even the dreaded state of widowhood – "Therefore humble yourselves under the mighty hand of God, that He may exalt you at the proper time, casting all your anxiety on Him, because He cares for you" (1 Pet. 5:6-7).

The only other restriction put on the widow in 1 Corinthians 7:39 limits whom she can marry to another Christian. *"A wife is bound as long as her husband lives; but if her husband is dead, she is free to be married to whom she wishes, only in the Lord"* (1 Cor. 7:39).

Notes

Notes

_____

_____

_____

_____

_____

_____

_____

_____

_____

_____

_____

_____

_____

_____

_____

_____

_____

_____

_____

_____

QUESTIONS:

1. What are the most likely concerns of young widows?_____

_____

_____

2. What are the most likely concerns of older widows?_____

_____

_____

3. What can we do to help both the younger and older widows? _____

_____

_____

4. What preparation can and should we do ahead of time in the event of our husband's death? _____

_____

_____

5. What restrictions and admonitions does the New Testament place on the widow and her family? _____

_____

_____

Facing Our Own Death

My heart is in anguish within me,
And the terrors of death have fallen upon me.
Fear and trembling come upon me,
And horror has overwhelmed me.
I said, "Oh, that I had wings like a dove!
I would fly away and be at rest.
Behold, I would wander far away,
I would lodge in the wilderness. Selah.
I would hasten to my place of refuge
From the stormy wind and tempest" (Psa. 55:4-8).

Whether we view our death as imminent or an event that will occur *some day*, it is a subject most of us don't like to think about and are reluctant to discuss with others. For that reason, some procrastinate in making out a will. Consciously or subconsciously, they feel by writing down their wishes for the disposition of their assets or making provision for their dependents, they are somehow hastening their demise.

King David spoke of death as a terror and a shadow. Most of us are at least wary of shadows, if not frightened by them. Children can see all kinds of monsters in the shape of shadows in their bedrooms. If you allay their fears about the shadows, then they may fear the monsters are hiding under their bed. They fear the unknown. As adults, we soothe their terrors with the light. We are not frightened by those shadows because we know there is nothing to be afraid of.

As the children of God, we should have that same trust in our heavenly Father, who has the power to allay our fears, dispel the darkness and reveal the shadows for what they are. We should

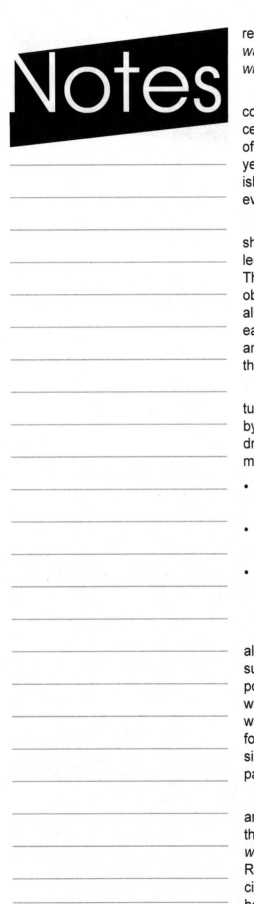

reach the point in our lives when we can say with David, *"Even though I walk through the valley of the shadow of death, I fear no evil, for You are with me; Your rod and Your staff, they comfort me"* (Psa. 23:4).

Death is one of the few certainties of life. The fact of death should not come as a surprise to us. God has given us ample warning as to the certainty of death both in nature and in Scripture. We observe the rhythm of life in animals and plants. Animals are born, live their allotted number of years, and then die. Plants spring up for a season or two and then perish. Some famous trees may live for a few hundred years, but they, too, eventually die.

In both the Old and New Testaments God has testified to mankind's shortness of life. We are even told in Genesis why this is so. Our benevolent Father put Adam and Eve in an environment where they need not die. They had access to a Tree of Life. They also had the ability to choose to obey God and live or listen to Satan and die. Unfortunately for us, Eve allowed Satan to trick her into disobeying God's express command not to eat of the Tree of Knowledge of Good and Evil. Adam followed Eve's example and also disobeyed God. Consequently, sin entered the world and they were banished from their perfect environment, the Garden of Eden.

The Scriptures speak of two kinds of death: physical death and spiritual death. Adam and Eve brought both kinds of death upon themselves by their disobedience. They were separated from God when they were driven out of their Garden – a spiritual death. Because of their sin, all men must now experience physical death.

- *"What man can live and not see death? Can he deliver his soul from the power of Sheol? Selah"* (Psa. 89:48).

- *"And inasmuch as it is appointed for men to die once and after this comes judgment"* (Heb. 9:27).

- *"Yet you do not know what your life will be like tomorrow. You are just a vapor that appears for a little while and then vanishes away"* (James 4:14).

If God had left it at that, the future would be dark indeed. However, our all-wise, all-knowing, all-powerful God, planned from the beginning for just such circumstances and did not leave mankind without hope. The whole point of separating the Jewish nation from the rest of the Old Testament world was to preserve a pure lineage from which the sinless Son of God would be born. He was to be the Savior of the world! The perfect sacrifice for sins! Jesus Christ was born into a sin-sick world to save us from our sins. He died on the cross, rose again, and ascended into heaven to prepare an eternal home for His consecrated people – Christians!

From the time of our conversion, we are preparing ourselves for death and that transition into life eternal. We are not left to wander aimlessly through life and hope we make it to heaven in the end. *"There is a way which seems right to a man, But its end is the way of death"* (Prov. 16:25). Rather, we are given a guide book, the Bible, the word of God, with specific instructions as to what we must do to become followers of Christ and how we are to live our lives. Mark 16:15,16 and Acts 2:38 are just two of many passages of Scripture that tell us how we are to become Christians:

- Believe in Christ as the Son of God
- Repent of our sins
- Confess Christ's name to others
- Be baptized for the remission of our sins.

The letters to the churches give instructions for life's journey. How we are to live, work, worship, raise our families, treat others, and our responsibilities to civil government. Armed with this knowledge, we should not be afraid of the transition from this life to the next one. We should not suffer the terrors of the unbeliever. *"The wicked is thrust down by his wrongdoing, But the righteous has a refuge when he dies"* (Prov. 14:32).

Death is the culmination of all our preparations. We endure trials and tribulations in this life while looking for that heavenly city where there shall be no more weeping, no more sickness, no more pain, no more disappointments, no more loneliness, no more darkness. (Please read Revelation 21 and 22.)

We should be able to say with Paul in Philippians 1:23, 24, *"But I am hard-pressed from both directions, having the desire to depart and be with Christ, for that is very much better; yet to remain on in the flesh is more necessary for your sake."* When we read of heaven in Revelation 21 and 22, we can understand why Paul felt it would be far better to depart the infirmities and persecutions in this life and go to be with Christ. Freed from the infirmities of the flesh we can fly away as David so eloquently pictured it. The body will return to the dust of the earth and our spirit will return back to God. What better place could we ask to be in?

So when this corruptible shall have put on incorruption, and this mortal shall have put on immortality, then shall be brought to pass the saying that is written, Death is swallowed up in victory. O death, where is thy sting? O grave, where is thy victory? The sting of death is sin; and the strength of sin is the law. But thanks be to God, which giveth us the victory through our Lord Jesus Christ (1 Cor. 15:54-57, KJV).

Notes

_____
_____
_____
_____
_____
_____
_____
_____
_____
_____
_____
_____
_____
_____
_____
_____
_____
_____
_____
_____

QUESTIONS:

1. Why do most people fear death?_____
_____
_____

2. Where did death originate? _____
_____

3. What happens to the soul of man when the body dies? _____
_____

4. What preparation has God made for His people upon their death?
_____
_____
_____

5. What preparation should we make for the day of our death? _____
_____
_____
_____

CPSIA information can be obtained
at www.ICGtesting.com
Printed in the USA
LVOW04s2314150218
566830LV00004B/7/P